Too Cute!

Baby Chickens

by Elizabeth Neuenfeldt

BLASTOFF!
Beginners

BELLWETHER MEDIA
MINNEAPOLIS, MN

Blastoff! Beginners are developed by literacy experts and educators to meet the needs of early readers. These engaging informational texts support young children as they begin reading about their world. Through simple language and high frequency words paired with crisp, colorful photos, Blastoff! Beginners launch young readers into the universe of independent reading.

Sight Words in This Book 🔍

a	come	have	the
and	eat	in	they
are	find	long	this
as	from	look	time
at	get	many	to
big	has	on	

This edition first published in 2023 by Bellwether Media, Inc.

No part of this publication may be reproduced in whole or in part without written permission of the publisher. For information regarding permission, write to Bellwether Media, Inc., Attention: Permissions Department, 6012 Blue Circle Drive, Minnetonka, MN 55343.

Library of Congress Cataloging-in-Publication Data

LC record for Baby Chickens available at: https://lccn.loc.gov/2022036381

Text copyright © 2023 by Bellwether Media, Inc. BLASTOFF! BEGINNERS and associated logos are trademarks and/or registered trademarks of Bellwether Media, Inc.

Editor: Betsy Rathburn   Designer: Jeffrey Kollock

Printed in the United States of America, North Mankato, MN.

Table of Contents

A Baby Chicken!   4

Tiny Hatchlings   6

Growing Up!   18

Baby Chicken Facts   22

Glossary   23

To Learn More   24

Index   24

A Baby Chicken!

Look at the
baby chicken.
Hello, chick!

Tiny Hatchlings

Chicks come from eggs. They start as **hatchlings**.

hatchling

egg

They are small.
They have
soft **feathers**.

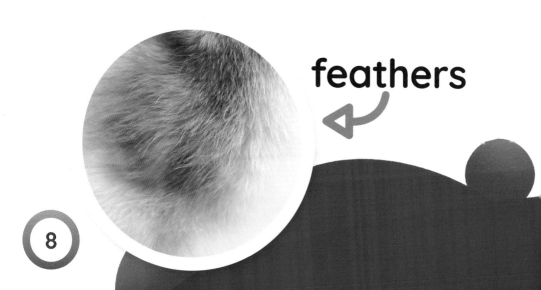

feathers

They live
on farms.
They sleep
in **coops**.

coop

Chicks have
many brothers
and sisters.

They stay
close to mom.
They stay warm.

mom

Chicks find food on the ground. They eat seeds and bugs.

bug

Growing Up!

Chicks get big.
They grow
a **wattle**.

wattle

This chick has long feathers. Time to fly!

Baby Chicken Facts

Chicken Life Stages

hatchling   chick   adult

A Day in the Life

sleep in a coop   stay close to mom   eat seeds and bugs

Glossary

coops

homes for chickens

feathers

soft coverings on chickens

hatchlings

chicks that were just born

wattle

red skin on a chicken's neck

To Learn More

ON THE WEB

FACTSURFER

Factsurfer.com gives you a safe, fun way to find more information.

1. Go to www.factsurfer.com.

2. Enter "baby chickens" into the search box and click 🔍.

3. Select your book cover to see a list of related content.

Index

big, 18
brothers, 12
bugs, 16, 17
chicken, 4
coops, 10
eat, 16
eggs, 6, 7
farms, 10
feathers, 8, 20

fly, 20
food, 16
grow, 18
hatchlings, 6, 7
mom, 14, 15
seeds, 16
sisters, 12
sleep, 10
small, 8

warm, 14
wattle, 18, 19